Quitting Marijuana

Your Personal Recovery Plan

SECOND EDITION

Cardwell C. Nuckols, Ph.D.

Acknowledgments

I would like to acknowledge the editorial expertise of Doug Toft,
whose contributions to this project were invaluable.

Hazelden
Center City, Minnesota 55012-0176

1-800-328-9000
1-651-213-4590 (Fax)
www.hazelden.org

©1992, 2003 by Hazelden Foundation
All rights reserved. First edition 1992
Second edition 2003
Printed in the United States of America

To request permission, write to Permissions Coordinator, Hazelden, P.O. Box 176, Center City, MN 55012-0176. To purchase additional copies of this publication, call 1-800-328-9000 or 1-651-213-4000.

ISBN: 1-59285-066-9

About the workbook

Using this workbook will help you create a personal plan to recover from marijuana addiction. One key to recovery is choosing new people, places, and things to be around. When you finish with this workbook, you will have a plan for recovery—one created by you—that will help you make the right choice.

About the author

Cardwell C. Nuckols, Ph.D., is president of Cardwell C. Nuckols and Associates. As a trainer and consultant, he works with hospitals, addiction treatment programs, community groups, industries, schools, and criminal justice systems throughout the country. His special interests are alcoholism, drug dependence, and behavioral medicine.

Cover design by Dave Spohn
Interior design and typesetting by Kinne Design

CONTENTS

How This Workbook Can Help You

It is often said that we don't ask much from people when they come into a treatment program for drug addiction. We only ask one thing: Change everything and do it now!

That sounds like a tall order—and it is. Fortunately, you don't have to do it all right now. Recovering from marijuana addiction is something you can work on for the rest of your life. Take it one Step and twenty-four hours at a time, and you will see your life turn around.

This workbook will support you in that effort. It has two main goals:

- *To make your recovery a positive experience.* Sure, recovery is not always fun. At times you might feel pretty bad. But recovery does not have to be that way all the time. Believe it or not, you can actually have fun in recovery.

  This workbook focuses on much more than just staying away from marijuana. It is also about doing new things instead of using—things you might really enjoy. After all, if recovery is going to be boring, why go through it?

- *To help you design a powerful plan for your recovery.* A powerful plan is personal and specific. That is, it's one that you shape and one that works for you. This kind of plan goes beyond general goals. For example, "go to self-help meetings" is a general goal. A specific action to reach that goal might be "go to Narcotics Anonymous (NA) meetings at church on Thursday evenings at seven and Saturday mornings at ten."

Success in recovery comes with changes in *doing* and *viewing*. As you begin to change your behavior, the "stinking thinking" that often comes with drug use will begin to fade. At first you might not understand why your behavior has to change, and you will act in new ways because that is what you have been told to do. Eventually, however, you will begin to understand why you must act differently. Your view of recovery and of the world around you will change. To put it simply: When you bring the body, the mind will follow.

Most of this workbook is about doing. It is full of exercises and tips. Underneath it all is one idea: When you are not using marijuana, you have control over what you do. This is true even when you start to crave marijuana or when you feel sad, fearful, or angry.

Most recovering people have heard the saying "If you do what you've always done, you'll get what you've always gotten." But it works the other way too. If you're doing changes, then your viewing will follow. You will start having new, better experiences.

How to Use This Workbook

Keep these points in mind as you go through this workbook:

- When you write what you plan to do, be specific. What will you do? Where? When? With whom? Can you do it today, or should you do something else first?

- Sometimes you might want to go back and change an answer. Write your answers in pencil so you can go back and erase.

- If you have trouble writing, then try drawing a picture or a chart that illustrates your answer to a question. Tape-record your responses, or explain your ideas to someone who can write down what you say.

One more thing: *Using this workbook is not a substitute for a treatment program.* Nor can it take the place of a self-help group. This workbook is designed for use with a counselor or a group leader who can assist you as you go through it. It can also be used to complement a variety of treatment programs: residential, outpatient, or continuing care.

AUTHOR'S NOTE

Certain tasks are common to recovery, no matter what the addiction. Nearly all the ideas presented in this workbook can apply to people recovering from alcohol or other drug addictions. However, the unique aspects of recovery from marijuana addiction are noted in the text.

Separate Myth from Reality

MYTH: *Marijuana is not addictive.*

REALITY: *Marijuana contains the potent drug delta-9-tetrahydrocannabinol (THC) that causes psychological and physical dependence.*

Studies on both animals and humans have documented the addictive properties of marijuana. Some human studies have shown that symptoms of withdrawal, one of the hallmarks of addiction, can occur within twenty-four hours of discontinuing use of the drug. These symptoms—which can include irritability, headache, aggression, anxiety, and difficulty sleeping—can last for five to seven days. Marijuana addicts who have experienced the initial withdrawal symptoms are often not prepared for the fact that many of these same symptoms can recur three to six weeks after their last use. Often these recurring symptoms are more severe and difficult to relate to earlier use. Addicts may feel like they are "losing it" and experience a strong craving for marijuana or another drug, such as alcohol, to medicate their symptoms.

MYTH: *Marijuana is pretty harmless.*

REALITY: *Marijuana is extremely potent and poses severe health risks.*

Marijuana use was long considered to be hazard free. Many people saw it as a "soft" drug and not as a potential health hazard.

Research shows that this lighthearted outlook on marijuana is naive. Marijuana has changed during the past three decades. From the late 1960s to the early 1970s, the THC content of marijuana was about 1 to 4 percent. Today marijuana can contain up to 17 percent THC or more. As a result, the intoxicated state achieved by marijuana users today is much more intense and long-lasting. Along with the greater high comes a greater chance of addiction.

MYTH: *Marijuana gives a pleasant, easy-to-control high.*

REALITY: *Marijuana's effects are hard to predict.*

Marijuana contains more than four hundred potentially active chemicals. This makes it hard to predict the effects of marijuana use. Marijuana intoxication differs drastically from person to person and from dose to dose.

One thing is certain: Marijuana is powerful. Nerve cells can be altered by as little as one-billionth of a gram of THC. Molecule for molecule, THC is not that much weaker than LSD and is actually much more potent than the hallucinatory drug mescaline. It takes only a very small dose of THC to disorient the brain.

Marijuana is also the only commonly abused drug that can enhance the high of other drugs such as alcohol and stimulants like cocaine and methamphetamine.

MYTH: *It is okay for marijuana addicts to continue to use alcohol or other drugs while in recovery.*

REALITY: *Whatever your drug of choice, use of any mood-altering chemical will undermine your recovery.*

Often marijuana addicts have alcohol or other drug problems. They might think they can give up marijuana but continue to drink or use cocaine. Similarly, addicts trying to give up cocaine or alcohol might say to themselves, *I will give up these drugs, but I can keep using marijuana.* In either case, the result of this bargaining is predictable: relapse.

Effects of Long-Term Marijuana Use

Following are some effects of long-term marijuana use.

Effects on the Heart

Marijuana can produce a rapid heart rate and high blood pressure. At times it can cause disturbances in heart rhythms. For marijuana smokers with normal hearts, this typically does not create a health hazard. However, if a user has any form of heart disease, marijuana use can be life threatening.

Effects on the Lungs

Chronic marijuana smokers tend to have sore throats, coughs, and sinus problems. They are more prone to bronchitis and pneumonia and generally have impaired immune systems. When a marijuana smoker damages lung tissue to the point that scar tissue forms, the damage is irreversible.

Marijuana smoke also contains some of the same cancer-causing compounds that are in cigarette smoke, and it shows a three- to five-times-higher absorption rate than that of tar and carbon monoxide. Just five marijuana cigarettes have an effect on the lungs equal to well over one-hundred tobacco cigarettes. Many marijuana smokers are also tobacco smokers, which means their chances for getting lung cancer and emphysema are greatly increased.

Effects on Sexuality

Men who use marijuana may have a reduced level of the male hormone testosterone and a reduced sperm count. They may also have abnormal sperm.

Females who are chronic users of marijuana may have irregular menstrual periods and may fail to ovulate (produce eggs). Women who smoke marijuana during pregnancy risk having a child with birth defects. Studies point to a higher probability of premature birth, low birth weight, sudden infant death syndrome (SIDS), childhood cancer, and an impairment of the brain's ability to think when children are regularly exposed to marijuana smoke prior to birth.

Adolescents who use marijuana risk altering their reproductive systems at a critical stage of physical growth. Secondary sexual features, such as voice pitch and development of body and facial hair, can be affected. Chronic users might develop sexual features more common to the opposite sex. This occurs because marijuana can alter the balance between male and female sex hormones.

Effects on Growth and Development

Marijuana use can disturb the way personalities develop. Denial, however, often keeps marijuana smokers from noticing these changes. For example, adolescence is an important time for learning how to get along with people and building higher-thinking skills. If using marijuana interrupts or distorts young people's development in these crucial areas, they will remain underdeveloped later in life. Still, marijuana users who started using as teens and who quit the drug in adulthood will often deny that their social and thinking problems have anything to do with their prior use.

Effects on Emotions

People are more likely to abuse marijuana when they are emotionally vulnerable. An adolescent or adult struggling with intense emotions and/or difficult life situations are more at risk to turn to marijuana as a form of relief. Marijuana abusers and addicts therefore don't learn to deal with difficult emotions and may experience a higher degree of inappropriate anger, anxiety, and depression as well as interpersonal and motivational problems.

Look at How Using Affects Your Life

Using marijuana alters your judgment and your reasoning ability, which makes it difficult to know whether the drug is affecting your performance in work or school. It is common for marijuana users to think that the drug helps them excel at certain tasks, but in reality, their performance usually declines.

How can you tell if you are abusing marijuana or are addicted to it? The best way is to look at what you and others can see: your behavior.

Looking at your behavior has another use: it helps you see how marijuana use changes your values. Consider the choice between studying for an exam and smoking marijuana, or the choice between making a car payment and buying marijuana. If you consistently choose marijuana, this says a lot about what has become most important to you.

 >> Complete Exercises 1 and 2

EXERCISE 1

Get the Facts about Your Marijuana Use

The following questions will help you see some ways marijuana use affects your life. Check either yes or no.

YES NO

☑ ☐ 1. Have you noticed that using marijuana makes music sound better, makes events or comments seem more humorous, and occasionally distorts your sense of time?

☑ ☐ 2. Have you purchased or been given marijuana for your own stash?

☑ ☐ 3. Are you regularly using marijuana to feel less angry and/or anxious?

☑ ☐ 4. Have you found yourself using marijuana at times other than social occasions?

☑ ☐ 5. Do you relate better to people who smoke marijuana than to people who don't use the drug?

☑ ☐ 6. Have you used marijuana before or during school or work?

☑ ☐ 7. Have you ever noticed while smoking marijuana that you cannot remember what you just read or were told?

☑ ☐ 8. If your answer to question 7 is yes, have you continued to use in those situations?

☑ ☐ 9. Have there been times when you were preoccupied with scoring marijuana?

☑ ☐ 10. When other people have frowned on your marijuana use (teachers, family members, employers, and so on), have you learned ways to get high without them knowing?

☑ ☐ 11. Have you felt anxious that others might know you were stoned?

☐ ☑ 12. Is it better to be stoned than it is to be straight at work, at school, or in social situations?

☑ ☐ 13. Do you sometimes think you would like to go through life without using marijuana?

YES   NO

☑   ☐   14. Does using marijuana cause you problems when driving a car or operating machinery?

☑   ☐   15. Have other people commented on one or more of the following: that you have changed who you hang out with, that your motivation has decreased, or that you have become less productive at work or school?

☐   ☐   16. If your answer to question 15 is yes, do you think that the problem is because of your old friends or because there is nothing worthwhile to motivate you, rather than being addicted to marijuana?

☐   ☑   17. Have you felt anxious or irritable or have you had headaches or difficulty sleeping when you went several days without smoking marijuana?

☑   ☐   18. Are there times when all you can think about is using marijuana or other drugs?

E X E R C I S E 2

Reflect on Your Marijuana Use

Has marijuana use kept you from getting anything you wanted in life? Write three examples here.

1. weed now

2.

3.

How would your life have been different without using marijuana? Name three goals you could have accomplished if you had been clean and sober.

1.

2.

3.

Make Your Own Plan for Recovery

There are three things to remember once you get into a recovery program: plan ahead, plan ahead, and plan ahead. That means choosing—in advance—how and when you will change the people, places, and things in your life.

Without a plan, it is easy to fall back into using. Someone who doesn't plan is trying to use the old willpower model to stay clean. The reasoning goes something like this: *If I'm tough enough and strong enough, I can just tough it out through recovery. I really don't have to change anything else about my life—I just won't use marijuana. Or I won't use for a while. Or I'll just cut down.*

But as you will learn in treatment or in your recovery group, willpower doesn't cut it. What is needed is an active strategy for recovery. If you want to succeed in recovery, make a plan. Then put the same amount of effort into your plan as you did into using.

Use a Problem-Solving Approach

Sometimes it is hard for addicts to solve basic problems in daily life. After all, they are used to a drug that "solves" any problem in a few seconds.

Fortunately, problem solving is a skill that improves with practice. As you seek to change the people, places, and things in your life, keep applying the following steps:

1. Define the problem.

2. Think of possible solutions.

3. Choose the most workable solution.

4. Write a list of "to dos" to accomplish that solution, and schedule a time for each item on the list.

5. Rehearse the solution in your mind.

Here is how these steps might apply to a specific situation. Say you are planning to attend your sister's wedding, which is scheduled for two weeks from today. You know that a cousin of yours who still smokes marijuana will be there. You also know there will be an open bar at the reception. Chances are your cousin will have a few drinks, then ask you to go outside to share a joint.

This is a potential problem—and an opportunity to plan. Grab a pencil and paper to make some notes. Then go through the five problem-solving steps:

1. *Define the problem.* The problem is that my cousin will ask me to smoke a joint with him at the reception, and it will be hard for me to say no to that request.

2. *Think of possible solutions.* (a) I could choose not to attend the wedding. (b) I could attend the wedding and not go to the reception. (c) I could take a friend from my NA group to the reception. By being there, he would remind me that recovery comes first. I could ask him to stick around while my cousin is there. I could make sure that my sister knows my plan.

3. *Choose the most workable solution.* Solution c sounds best. It allows me to attend the wedding and the reception. At the same time, it greatly increases my chances of staying sober.

4. *Write a list of "to dos" to accomplish that solution, and schedule a time for each item on the list.* To carry out this solution, I will make two phone calls: one to my sister and another to my recovering friend. I will call my sister tonight, and I will call my recovering friend this weekend.

5. *Rehearse the solution in your mind.* During the week before the reception, I will run some "videos" in my head. I will see myself at the reception with my NA friend. We will be laughing, eating, enjoying being with people. My cousin will strike up a conversation. When that happens, I will introduce him to my recovering friend. Instead of smoking with my cousin, I will make a point of seeking out other relatives I haven't seen for a while.

That's it. Now you have a powerful, specific plan for heading off a potential problem.

Keep this approach in mind as you continue with the exercises in this workbook. Each exercise can help you chart a positive recovery course. If you act on your plans, *you* will start to run the people, places, and things in your life—instead of letting them run you. You will also begin to master problem solving, a skill that will serve you for a lifetime.

Change People, Places, and Things That Promote Drug Use

Why do people keep using marijuana, even after treatment? Usually because there is a failure to change the *people, places,* and *things* that promote drug use. For example, take the person who has just left a treatment program. He intends to stay clean. Before long, though, he starts seeing the same friends he knew when he was smoking a lot of marijuana—people who still use the drug. He also starts going to concerts in places where he used to smoke. Beyond that, there are still marijuana-related paraphernalia in his apartment. Each of these people, places, and things is a roadblock to recovery.

Compare this to another person, also just out of treatment, who seeks out new, clean-and-sober friends. She finds a sponsor and calls that person at least once each week at a scheduled time. She goes to NA meetings regularly.

After each meeting, she makes a point of talking to someone with more experience in recovery. There are no drug paraphernalia in her home. Instead she has recovery-related reading materials. This person is supporting her recovery in specific, powerful ways. Her life will show the results.

 >> Complete Exercises 3 through 13

EXERCISE 3

Find a Role Model

In the past you might have found yourself selecting friends and social events that allowed you to use. Perhaps you excluded people from your life who did not smoke marijuana.

Compile a list of people you know—people who are generally happy, loving, and skilled at making and keeping friends. They do not have to be people in recovery, but they must be people who do not abuse chemicals. Think of family and church members, friends, and people you have met in treatment or in your self-help group. List the names of positive people who could serve as role models for you.

Look over the names you listed. Circle the name of one person you could contact in the next week.

How will you contact this person (letter, e-mail, phone call, self-help meeting)? Write in the space provided.

When will you make this contact? Note a specific time.

EXERCISE 4

Choose the People You'll Spend Time With

List the names of people you spent a lot of time with when you used marijuana.

Are any of these people still using? Circle their names.

Are you likely to come into contact with any of these people? List the names of the people you might run across.

What will you do or say if you meet one of these people and he or she suggests using? Write some specific ideas in the following space.

Would it be a good idea *not* to see some of these people? List their names.

Now recall the positive relationships you had before you started using. Think of relatives or friends who meant a lot to you, whether you have seen them lately or not. List their names.

Just as you did in exercise 3, choose one name from the list—a person you could contact within the next week. How will you contact that person? Write your plan in the space provided.

EXERCISE 5

Find a Self-Help Group

Are you attending any self-help groups such as Narcotics Anonymous or Alcoholics Anonymous? List those groups here.

If you are not attending any self-help groups, then do you know of any in your area? List them here.

Do you know where and when these groups meet? If so, list the names and locations for each group. (If you don't know of meetings, check the phone book or, if available, an AA, NA, or other directory.) List a contact number and/or person for each group and write that information next to the group listing.

If you do not know of any groups in your area, then who can help you find that information? List some names here.

Choose one name to begin with. How and when will you contact this person?

Work with a Sponsor

Think again of recovering people you know. These might include people in treatment or people you have met in a self-help group. List their names.

Choose one person you would like as a sponsor. (If you already have a sponsor, go on to the next question.) This should ideally be someone with whom there is no danger of having a sexual relationship, who has solid sobriety (two years or more), and who works a good program. How and when will you contact this person to discuss the idea? Write out your plan of action.

Do you already have a sponsor? If so, list this person's name and phone number here.

Are you talking with your sponsor regularly, either by phone or in person? If so, when do you talk?

If you are not talking regularly with a sponsor, make a plan to do so. What are times you could talk to your sponsor? List at least three options here.

1.

2.

3.

When will you call your sponsor to discuss these possible meeting times and to set up a regular schedule?

EXERCISE 7

Consider Counseling

As you read earlier, using marijuana can subtly affect the way you think and feel. Getting professional counseling can help you see the big picture about your use. Also, other emotional problems or disorders unrelated to your addiction can be hidden by your use. Would professional counseling be useful to you? If so, who could provide that counseling or help you find a counselor? List at least three options here.

1.

2.

3.

Now choose one name from the list. How and when will you contact this person?

Do you need help making arrangements for counseling, such as figuring out how you will pay, getting rides to the sessions, and so on? If so, list the name of someone who could help you with these problems.

When and how will you contact this person?

EXERCISE 8

Find Alternatives to the Places Where You Used

Most marijuana smokers use in private as well as public places. You might have used at home in the mornings or evenings, or perhaps in your car. You might have used in a parking lot at work or school.

List the places where you most often smoked marijuana.

Underline the places you *can* avoid during your early recovery. Circle the places you *cannot* avoid.

Now imagine yourself with a chance to use in one of those places you circled. What can you say or do to avoid using? List each place you circled; then write down some phrases you could say or actions you could take.

What can you do in these places instead of using? List at least three options here.

1.

2.

3.

EXERCISE 9

Plan for Connection and Fun

List some recreational activities you enjoyed before you started using marijuana, especially those activities that connected you with other people. Think of the things enjoyed by people in recovery or anyone else with a healthy lifestyle (for example, playing sports or music, doing volunteer work, participating in church functions). List several activities here and on the next page.

Look at the list you just wrote. Circle the activities you would enjoy doing now.

Now choose one of the activities you circled. If you want to do this activity, what steps would you need to take? List the activity and the steps you would take. Who would you need to contact? What equipment or materials would you need?

Which of these steps can you complete in the coming week? List them here, along with a specific time for doing each of them.

EXERCISE 10

Plan for Nutrition and Exercise

Most marijuana users know about the "munchies"—sudden strong cravings for food. They also know how easy it is to satisfy these cravings with foods that are high in sugar or fat.

Making a recovery plan gives you a chance to look at the way you eat. This is an excellent time to make changes in your diet that will promote your recovery. Eating habits, changes in moods, and cravings for marijuana are all related. Making a positive change in one of these areas can affect the others as well.

Think about your diet as it relates to using marijuana. For instance, did you tend to skip meals when you were high? Did you eat more sweets, junk foods, and fast foods, such as potato chips, ice cream, candy bars, sodas? Describe how using marijuana affects the way you eat.

Does smoking marijuana affect how much nicotine or caffeine you consume? Explain how.

Now list one or two changes you intend to make in the way you eat or drink (for example, switching to low-fat foods, drinking decaffeinated coffee). Remember to keep it simple.

When you crave snacks, are there activities you could substitute for eating? For example, instead of eating a dessert or drinking a cup of coffee after dinner, could you go for a walk or call a friend? List one or two activities that would work for you.

Are you exercising regularly? If so, describe your exercise routine here.

If you are not exercising regularly, list some possible forms of exercise you could start within the next week. (Remember to check with a doctor before starting any rigorous exercise program.)

Now choose one type of exercise that would be fun for you. List it here.

What steps can you take to begin this activity? For example, do you need equipment, supplies, or training? How will you get those things?

What exactly will you do? When? Where? With whom?

Plan for Staying Sober at School or Work

Recall the times you used marijuana at school or work. Did you smoke a joint on the way to school or work? Did you smoke in a parking lot? Did you stop by a bar after work and then use marijuana in your car before driving home?

Make a plan now to change your activities during these times. For example, exercise during the lunch hour and eat a light lunch just before you are due back in class or at your job. Avoid parking near the places where people are dealing or using. If possible, change your route so you don't go past any bars.

List two or three such strategies here. Choose ones that support your recovery.

Now choose one activity to start in the next week. Describe what you will do and when you will do it.

Do you have access to an employee assistance program or a student assistance program? If so, work through your strategies with a counselor from that program. Make an appointment with that counselor this week. Put your plan in writing here.

EXERCISE 12

Plan for Staying Sober with Family

Did you often use marijuana after certain family events? For example, did you crave the drug after a fight with your spouse or partner or children? Did you use in order to feel more comfortable at family reunions? Describe any such events here.

What can you do now to change the way you think or feel about those events you listed? Think of some options. For example, can you take a course to sharpen your listening skills? Can you discuss family problems with a family counselor or a friend? List your options here.

From the actions you listed, choose one that you can complete in the next month. Step by step, describe exactly what you will do and when you will do it.

Plan for How to Deal with Cravings for Marijuana

Many sights, sounds, smells, or thoughts can trigger cravings for marijuana. For many addicts, getting stoned and listening to certain music go together naturally. Thus, hearing certain music can bring on the urge to use.

You cannot directly control the strength of any craving you might feel for marijuana. However, you can control your *response* to a craving. Develop a detailed picture in your mind about what to do if you feel a craving.

Keep the following points in mind:

- It is normal to feel cravings.
- Cravings don't last. They will pass. A craving often feels most intense just before it starts to fade.
- If you give in to a craving to use marijuana, the next craving could be stronger. If you don't give in to cravings to use marijuana, the cravings should become weaker over time.

Now plan how you will deal with cravings for marijuana. For the next few days, pay attention to any cravings you have. Answer the following questions:

When did you feel cravings? List specific times.

Where were you when you felt cravings?

What were you doing when you felt cravings?

Now look at the big picture. Do you see patterns in your cravings? For example, do you feel more intense cravings on certain days or at certain times? Do certain people, places, or things seem associated with strong cravings? Describe here any patterns you see.

Now decide how you want to respond to cravings. Here are some ideas that have worked for other recovering people:

- Write a brief message to give to yourself when you feel a craving. Choose a prayer, slogan, or quotation with special meaning for you. Make sure it is positive and recovery-oriented. Memorize this message and recite it silently or aloud, or write the message on a three-by-five-inch index card and carry it with you.

- Take a specific action when you feel a craving. If certain music triggers cravings for you, then play different music. Choose an action that is easy to do in a variety of times and places. For example, some people find it helps during a craving to take long, slow, deep breaths.

- Call to mind a specific time when you felt your recovery was going exception-ally well. Pretend you made a videotape of that situation. In your mind, play back the videotape. Where were you, and who were you with? What were you doing? What were you saying? What thoughts were running through your mind? Recall as many details as you can. Make the picture in your mind as bright and colorful as possible.

- Carry with you a small picture of someone you love. Choose someone with a stake in your recovery: a spouse, partner, child, parent, or friend. Look at this picture whenever you feel cravings. Doing so reminds you that the reasons for staying sober involve others as well as yourself.

Now think of some things you can do when you feel cravings. List at least six possibilities here.

1.

2.

3.

4.

5.

6.

Choose one option to try for a week. Describe exactly what you will do.

How did this option work for you? Do you want to continue the technique you used? If not, choose another technique to try and describe it here.

Keep a Journal

The best plans are written plans. Writing helps focus your thoughts like nothing else. When your recovery plan is down on paper, you can add to it, change it, and refine it.

Keeping a journal is popular among many recovering people. This activity gives you regular access to your most powerful thoughts. In fact, a journal is like having a sponsor who is available twenty-four hours a day.

You don't have to write well to keep a journal. Nobody else needs to read it. Write every day, but remember there is no specific format you have to follow. Just do what works.

Here are some ways to get started on your journal:

- List your recovery "to dos." A typical entry might be "Three things I need to do to stay sober today." Before you go to sleep, review your list and jot down some thoughts for the next day.

- Keep lists: gratitude lists, inventories, or amends you have made or need to make.

- One month from now go through the exercises in this workbook again. Write your new responses in your journal. Doing so updates your recovery plan.

- Write out prayers, meditations, and slogans you like, or create your own.

- Sum up key insights about recovery that you have discovered from reading books, listening to tapes, or talking with other recovering people.

Start now. On a separate piece of paper, begin a journal entry, following one of the suggestions given above.

 >> Complete Exercise 14

Sum Up Your Plan

To bring your recovery plan into even sharper focus, reread what you have written in this workbook. Review the text and exercises. See if there are any themes you can identify. Chances are, some ideas and actions come up more than others. It is worth noting these.

After reviewing this workbook, list the three most important things you have learned about yourself.

1.

2.

3.

Now list the three most important actions you can take as part of your recovery plan. These are actions you intend to carry out *no matter what.*

1.

2.

3.

Review this list from time to time to make sure your recovery plan is on track. Then savor all the positive changes that recovery is bringing to your life.

Sustain Your Plan

Recovery is not rocket science. It doesn't require a Ph.D. In fact, recovery is well within anyone's reach—including yours.

As you probably discovered in doing the exercises, there is nothing earth-shattering about the material in this workbook. All you need to do is put some basic ideas into practice. As the old slogan reminds us, "Keep it simple."

People falter in recovery when they make it too complicated. This workbook attempts to break down recovery into simple changes in behavior. Carry out those changes, and you will see a real difference in how you think and feel.

It is also important to keep your focus positive. That means centering on the dos instead of the don'ts. If you dwell on all the things you used to do that you can't do anymore, then it is easy to feel deprived. But if you focus on all the new activities you can do in recovery—as well as all the old pain you have been avoiding—things start to look up.

Recovery might not be easy, but it can be simple. You don't need to carry around a lot of new information. What really works is making simple changes in your doing and your viewing.

Following are five tips to help you sustain your recovery plan. They sum up the main points in this workbook, and they will point you toward success in recovery—and in life, for that matter.

Five Tips for Keeping Your Recovery Plan Alive

Tip 1: Develop a clear picture of recovery

People just starting in recovery might not have a clear picture of their new lifestyle. They know they want to stay clean and sober, but what does that look like on a Tuesday afternoon at three o'clock? What will they do, say, and think differently? If you have done the exercises in this workbook, you already have lots of answers to these questions. You have started to bring your own picture of recovery into clear focus.

Tip 2: Be willing to change

There are no secrets to recovery. It gets down to a few questions: What do I want? What price am I willing to pay for it? Am I willing to change the people, places, and things in my life?

That sounds harsh, but notice the wording of that tip: Be *willing* to change. As the Big Book of AA points out, what we need is the honesty, openness, and willingness to start changing. In time, the rest will follow.

Tip 3: Stay around positive people

Millions of people have walked the well-lit highway of recovery before you. What's more, many of them are willing to walk with you right now. When you go to self-help meetings, attend counseling, or see your sponsor, you are involving other people in your recovery. This is one of the most powerful things you can do. There is no need to go it alone. Reach out. Ask for support.

Tip 4: Keep learning about recovery

Many people in treatment read a few pages of the Big Book, but after they are out of treatment, they fail to read anything more about recovery. It is far more effective to keep reading, listening, and speaking with people about recovery.

Keep in mind the saying "What you think about expands." Flood your mind with recovery thoughts, and your recovery will start to expand in healthy directions.

What if you spent one hour a day for five days with recovery-related materials? You would know more about the subject than many recovering people! Do this several times a year, and watch the rewards come your way.

Tip 5: Keep doing what works

An old story about a recovering addict and his sponsor reinforces the importance of doing what works. It seems the addict lost both his family and his job on the same day. That evening, in despair, he contacted his sponsor and explained what had happened. His sponsor listened with great understanding. All he said was "Don't use, keep going to meetings, and this too shall pass."

Although the addict didn't fully understand, he managed to apply this advice, even through some grim times. After a while his life started to turn around. He gave up his resentments and fears. He started forgiving other people. He became sharper, more clearheaded, more competent. Eventually, he reunited with his family and returned home. What's more, his old employer hired him back with a hefty increase in pay.

Bursting with pride, the addict told his sponsor what had happened. His sponsor listened with great understanding. Then all he said was "Don't use, keep going to meetings, and this too shall pass."

Life in recovery sometimes feels like an emotional roller coaster. It is easy to get stopped by the lows and get attached to the highs. Sticking to a basic recovery plan helps us ride the ups and downs with growing serenity.

■